hip ...

HOORAY!

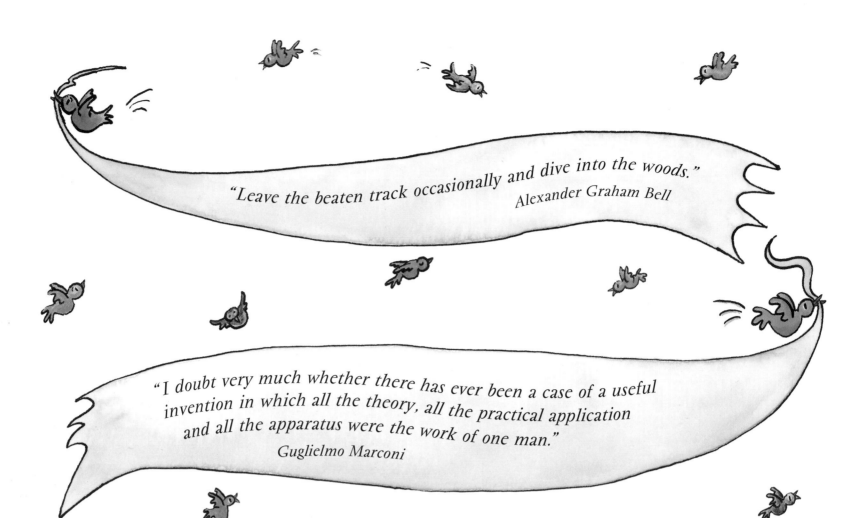

"Leave the beaten track occasionally and dive into the woods."
Alexander Graham Bell

" I doubt very much whether there has ever been a case of a useful invention in which all the theory, all the practical application and all the apparatus were the work of one man."
Guglielmo Marconi

First published 2005 by Walker Books Ltd
87 Vauxhall Walk, London SE11 5HJ

This edition published 2006

10 9 8 7 6 5 4 3 2 1

© 2005 Marcia Williams

The right of Marcia Williams to be identified as author/illustrator of this work has been asserted by her in accordance with the Copyrights, Designs and Patents Act 1988

This book has been typeset in Vendome

Printed in China

British Library Cataloguing in Publication Data: a catalogue record for this book is available from the British Library

ISBN 10: 1-4063-0171-X
ISBN 13: 978-1-4063-0171-7

www.walkerbooks.co.uk

THREE CHEERS
FOR
INVENTORS!

Written and illustrated by

Marcia Williams

WALKER BOOKS
AND SUBSIDIARIES
LONDON · BOSTON · SYDNEY · AUCKLAND

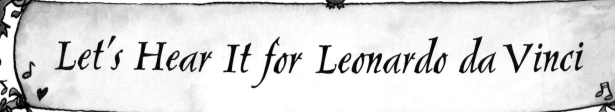

Let's Hear It for Leonardo da Vinci

THIS BOOK IS DEDICATED TO MY
SPECIAL HERO OF INVENTION,

Leonardo da Vinci

♥ (1452 ~ 1519) ♥

So, what
did he
invent?

Cast your
eyes yonder
and you will
see a few of
the many
inventions.

LEONARDO DA VINCI was born in Italy during the Renaissance, a time of learning and creativity. He was a brilliant artist and a great inventor, though many of his inventions were so advanced that they would have to be reinvented hundreds of years later when technology had caught up with them. Some of Leonardo's inventions were inspired by his study of nature, such as his aeroplane with flapping wings. He produced beautiful technical drawings of his experiments and observations; these still astound and inspire scientists today. Leonardo was also a gentle, peace-loving vegetarian, who bought caged birds just for the joy of setting them free!

THANK YOU, SIGNOR DA VINCI, FOR YOUR INSPIRATION!

Thank you,
Signor da Vinci,
for our freedom!

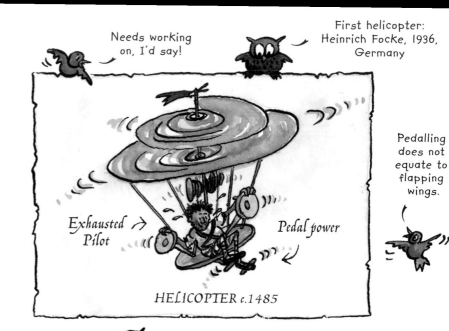
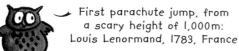

All Praise the Reader!

I thought we were praising inventors!

Readers are important too!

There would be no readers without inventors.

First alphabet: Phoenicians, c.1700 BC

There would be no date today without the inventors of yesterday.

Calendar: Ancient Rome, 45 BC

Dear Reader,

This is a book about my favourite inventors, my personal heroes and heroines of invention. Before I started writing this book, I imagined that inventors were boring, eccentric scientists who never left their laboratories. I was wrong. Inventors come in all shapes, sizes, sexes and ages, and they are brilliant. Well, most of them are brilliant!

Inventors don't just discover things that have always been there but went unnoticed; they create things that are entirely new. They see a need for something and then work away until they find the solution, although not all inventors are totally original. Some take an invention that isn't working very well and reinvent it so that it works superbly and everybody wants it! An invention that nobody wants soon gets forgotten, while other inventions change our lives for ever.

Every generation has had inventors. Every generation will have inventors. Perhaps there is an inventor lurking inside you. Without inventors, we might still be living in the Stone Age.

THREE CHEERS FOR INVENTORS!
I hope you enjoy reading about them.

Marcia Williams

P.S. If you do become an inventor, don't forget to patent your information. A patent will stop other inventors from stealing your idea and gives you the sole right to make and sell your invention.

P.P.S. The words the inventors and others use in this book are not their own. I have taken the liberty of imagining what they might have said.

So, who are the chosen inventors?

Do I need to know?

Allow us to present

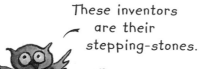
Why aren't there more modern inventors listed?

These inventors are their stepping-stones.

Without the radio, no TV ...

Without the TV, no video ...

Without the video, no DVD.

Contents

We don't want DVDs ... we like videos.

You two have no sense of adventure.

Just think where a DVD might lead to...

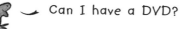

Can I have a DVD?

Here we go ... consumer-itus!

Pi Sheng from China invented moveable type in 1041 AD.

Well, it never reached Europe, so it needed reinventing!

Lucky for him, paper had been invented!

Paper: 105 AD, China

Ink: 2500 BC, China and Egypt

Can owls do jokes or just facts?

Inventions don't come cheap!

Cheap! Cheap! Cheap!

Hooray for Johannes Gutenberg (1400~1468) and his Moveable Type

Tell me the story of Noah's Ark, again.

I can't remember it.

I can't sleep without a story. You should've written it down.

That would take much too long.

When Johannes was growing up in Mainz, Germany, nobody read him a bedtime story, because there were no books to read.

Only monks have the time to write down stories.

INK MADE OF GALL NUT GROWTHS FOUND ON OAK TREES

Please could you write down a bedtime story for me?

Certainly, just wait twenty years while I finish copying the Bible.

MONK WITH LOTS OF TIME AND GOOD EYESIGHT!

The only book Johannes ever saw was the Bible. He would watch the monks at the local monastery copying it out by hand. The only method of printing known then was woodblock printing and that was very slow.

Stop dreaming of stories! Be a goldsmith like me.

There are lots and lots of stories in the Bible.

If I can make many coins, why not many moveable letters – I could use them to print a Bible quickly!

Johannes trained as a goldsmith and went to work in the mint, where coins were struck.

While he stamped out the coins, he had the idea of casting individual letters for printing in a similar way.

Why is my purse always empty?

Wow, thanks!

You can pay us back when you're rich and famous.

Stop, it's my invention!

Well, we want to be rich and famous.

But the tools, inks and metals he needed were very expensive.

For a time, three bankers helped him out with money.

Then one died and the other two tried to steal his plans.

10

If purses hadn't been invented, they couldn't be empty.

If my tummy hadn't been invented, it couldn't be empty.

Can you imagine a world without books?

Quite well, actually.

You are just an illiterate philistine.

My dreams are in tatters.

Johannes was forced to give up his experiments.

As much as you want. Pay me back when you're rich and famous.

Really?

Then Johann Fust, a lawyer, lent him the money to start again.

I'm ready! The moment has come to print the first Gutenberg Bible.

By 1450, Johannes had cast the letters and prepared a press.

Before you begin I'd like my money back, PLUS a lot of interest, NOW!

You're joking!

But then, Fust asked for his money back, plus interest!

My purse is empty.

You must have something of value.

Poor Johannes had spent it all on the press.

Ah, yes, your press. Thank you, my dear fellow.

No!

He was forced to hand over his press and work for Fust.

More ink coming up, Mr Gutenberg!

I'll have to learn to read now, Mr Gutenberg!

Those are my Bibles!

PAGES WAITING FOR BINDING

INK AS USED BY PAINTERS!

FORME FOR ARRANGING LETTERS

METAL LETTERS

PRESS ADAPTED FROM OLIVE OR GRAPE PRESS

VELLUM BEING STRETCHED

Yes, but now the stories belong to everyone.

Will you read me a story?

But Johannes still achieved his childhood dream. In 1456, while employed by Fust, he started to print his first Bible. It could take a monk up to thirty years to make one copy of the Bible. In one year, Johannes had printed 300 copies! By 1500, there were printers all over Europe and they had printed 30,000 books. As a result, knowledge and the changes that it brings spread with increasing speed.

What he needs is a patent!

Bird-brain. Modern patents weren't invented until 1625.

Owls think they are so clever.

I'm not in a position to comment.

Three cheers for the Gutenberg Bible!

It was an information revolution!

Imagine having to learn to read.

The mind boggles.

THANKS, JAMES WATT (1736–1819), for the SEPARATE STEAM CONDENSER

James Watt was born in Greenock, a small Scottish fishing village. He was a clever lad, but too sickly to go to school, so he stayed at home mending, making and tinkering with this and that.

When he did go to school, he was a top pupil but his attendance was very poor.

Eventually, James got a job at Glasgow University making and repairing scientific instruments.

One day, a friend brought him a model of a Newcomen steam engine to mend.

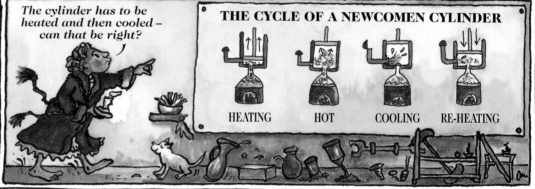

THE CYCLE OF A NEWCOMEN CYLINDER

HEATING   HOT   COOLING   RE-HEATING

James had heard of this engine. It was named after its inventor, Thomas Newcomen, and was used for pumping water out of mines. It was a brilliant idea but it did not work very efficiently.

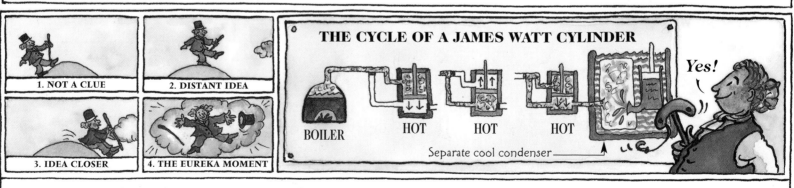

1. NOT A CLUE   2. DISTANT IDEA

3. IDEA CLOSER   4. THE EUREKA MOMENT

THE CYCLE OF A JAMES WATT CYLINDER

BOILER   HOT   HOT   HOT

Separate cool condenser

Yes!

James went for a little walk and a big think. Before long, he realized that he could improve the engine by making a separate cool container in which the steam would condense on its own.

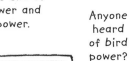

Eleven years is but a blink of the eye to me.

It's probably nearer two bird lifetimes.

This is the end of horse power and water power.

Anyone heard of bird power?

ELEVEN	YEARS	IS	A	VERY
LONG	TIME	TO	HAVE	TO	WAIT.

But James could not raise the money to build it. He worked at jobs he hated for over eleven years.

At last, he met a businessman, Matthew Boulton, and they formed a partnership.

You must be joking. It's steam, steam, steam from now on.

Too much steam! I can't breathe!

It's an industrial revolution.

They finally made the James Watt engine in 1776. It worked brilliantly, used less fuel than the Newcomen engine, and the miners stayed a lot drier! The new steam engine soon began to make other industries, such as the manufacture of cotton, quicker and more efficient. Watt kept on improving his steam engine until he was so rich he did not have to work any more. Then he thought he might invent a moving steam engine, but he decided he would rather go back to mending, making and tinkering with this and that.

Steam was used to power factories...

And cars, boats, heating, etc., etc.

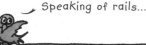

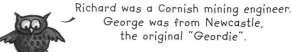
Actually, the Ancient Greeks shifted theatre scenery on rails.

Richard was a Cornish mining engineer. George was from Newcastle, the original "Geordie".

Toot-Toot-Toot-Toot
for Richard Trevithick (1771–1833)
and George Stephenson (1781–1848)
and the STEAM RAILWAY

Cast-iron rails were invented in 1763; steel ones in 1858.

Is it painful being a know-it-all?

Boys and their toys!

Luckily, the portable fire pump was invented in 1699.

Horse-drawn railways are quieter.

And pongier!

Out you go. You are too slow, too obstinate and too big!
Yes, sir!

I want to be a wrestler.
No, Son, it's the mines for you.

Faster, my baby.

Unlike James Watt, Richard Trevithick dreamt of steam transport. He left school early and went into the mines with his father. There he worked on the steam engines used to drag wagons of coal on rails.

I need to work on the steering.

One of us needs to lose weight.

Richard built a small high-pressure steam carriage on wheels, but it ran into a house!
Then in 1803, he built a steam locomotive that ran on cast-iron mining rails, but the rails broke.

ONE PENNY
A RIDE
ON THE TREVITHICK
STEAM ENGINE
CATCH ME WHO CAN

Is this a new breed of horse?
It's a wild beast!
It's the work of Satan.
SAY NO TO LOCOS!

Four years later, he built a lighter locomotive that pulled passenger wagons around a circular track. It caused a lot of excitement. But Richard failed to raise the money to develop the idea. Eventually, he gave up the struggle and went to be a mining engineer in Peru.

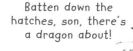
Batten down the hatches, son, there's a dragon about!

Speed can be fatal.

14

My miner's lamp. Note the glass chimney to prevent an explosion if there's gas about.

Great stuff.

A younger man, George Stephenson, took up the challenge. George had worked around mines from an early age. He had designed a miner's safety lamp and was a whizz at improving the power of steam engines. He wanted steam locomotives to replace horse-drawn tramways.

Lay me some railway tracks!

Oh, I will and it won't be horse-drawn wagons that run on them.

SAY NO TO LOCO-MOTION

NO LOCOS NO

GEORGE IS LOCO!

HORSES ARE BEST!

STEAM RAILWAY PLAN 1A

His chance came when he was employed by Edward Pease, a businessman who wanted goods transported between Stockton and Darlington.

LOCOMOTION

DARLINGTON

HOPE

STOCKTON

By 1825, George had two steam locomotives, *Locomotion* and *Hope*, plus a passenger carriage called *Experiment*, running between the two towns.

I could become a speed freak!

I've done it, Son. I've invented a locomotive and a railway!

We've done it, Dad!

You hitching a ride?

Cheap!

Chuff chuff! Into the future.

WATER FOR TURNING INTO STEAM

TENDER FOR COAL

1829

FIRE BOX

BOILER WITH 25 HEATING TUBES

ROCKET

Then in 1829, George and his son, Robert, won a competition with the *Rocket*, which travelled unloaded at the unheard-of speed of 56 kph (35 mph). It convinced the government that a steam railway should go ahead. By 1838, George's railway was running so efficiently that he was able to retire. But he never stopped inventing and always travelled by rail!

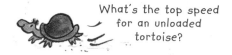

Did someone mention food and rest?

First rail restaurant carriage: 1863, USA
First sleeping carriage: 1865, USA

First US railway line: 1828

First US locomotive: Tom Thumb, 1830

Singing through the mountains, Buzzing o'er the vale. Bless me, this is pleasure, A-riding on a rail.

Finally, a less well-known Stephenson invention: the straight cucumber!

Poor Thomas. He began to go deaf when he was thirteen.

What? Tweet up, please!

That bird's cuckoo!

Snore!

He became known as "the wizard" because he invented so many things.

Like what?

Well, a moving picture machine, a talking doll, a flame-thrower...

What about the telegraph?

No, that was Claude Chappe, 1793, France. It was replaced by the electric telegraph: Samuel Morse, 1842, USA.

Dot ... dot ... dash.

He'll start another fire, you mark my words.

LIGHT UP FOR THOMAS EDISON (1847–1931)

LATEST NEWS, SWEETEST SWEETS!

ME! ME!

In 1859, twelve-year-old American Thomas Edison was earning a living selling sweets and newspapers on the Ohio railway line. He enjoyed a healthy profit!

I want those poisons out of my house!

But they are harmless.

You'd think that I was going to blow the place up!

Thomas loved science and had a laboratory at home until he had to move it to a railway carriage.

Oops!

GO AND DON'T BOTHER TO COME BACK!

Unfortunately, within weeks the carriage had been burnt to the ground and Thomas had lost his job.

Time to make a move!

He was not out of work for long, as shortly afterwards he saved a little boy from an oncoming train.

Mr Morse has invented a code of short and long signals to tap out messages on this machine.

So that's how you know when a train is due.

As a reward, the boy's father taught him Morse code and how to use the electric telegraph.

No, sir'ee, you won't see my hand move 'cos I'm the fastest operator in the USA!

Thomas quickly became a super-fast operator and was able to travel and work all over America.

Now, if I just unscrew this ...

add a bit of this ...

put this here...

But he was more interested in selling his ideas for improving the telegraph and similar machines.

If you want to work for me, forget sleep!

Of course, sir – snore!

By 1869, he had made enough money to set up an inventing business at Menlo Park, New Jersey.

16

What's the betting he'll invent a way to keep 'em awake?

What, like a night light?

It was a brilliant time to be an inventor. With a team of assistants, Thomas set about inventing and even taking orders for inventions.

In 1877, he invented the amazing phonograph. It was a forerunner of the record-player and recorded sound on a metal cylinder.

But his chief ambition was electric light for every home! For that, he first needed to improve the light bulb invented by the Englishman, Joseph Swan. It took a while but Thomas finally succeeded.

Electric light was safer, brighter and cleaner than gas lamps, and to prove it, in 1879, Thomas gave a public New Year's Eve party. Three thousand people arrived in the dark ... then the lights were switched on! The party was a great success, and everyone left convinced that electric light was better than gas. Thomas went on to design complete electrical systems. Even then, he did not stop to rest but went on and on inventing. He was a true businessman-inventor.

Put Your Hands Together for Inventors of Useful Things

Sorry!

Left margin notes:

Hands were invented as people have no beaks!

Can-opener: Robert Yeates, 1855, Britain

Flush toilet: John Harrington, 1591, Britain

He made quite a splash!

The Romans also invented mouthwash made out of urine!

Yuck!

Antiseptics: Ignaz Semmelweis, 1847, Hungary

PHILIBERT DE L'ORME:
Concrete, 1568, France

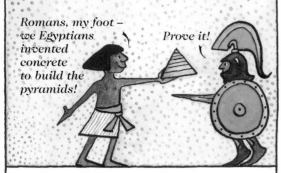

Romans, my foot – we Egyptians invented concrete to build the pyramids!

Prove it!

Concrete was invented by the Romans c. 200 BC. The architect Philibert rediscovered it.

PETER DURAND:
Tin Can, 1810, Britain

Mess up!

BEANS

SOUP

You needed a hammer and chisel to open early tin cans!

WALTER ALCOCK:
Toilet Paper on a Roll, 1882, Britain

Help!

Come and get it.

Not guilty!

LADISLAO BIRO: Ballpoint Pen, 1938, Hungary

WOW

More than 14 million ballpoint pens are sold everyday!

THE GOOD OLD ROMANS: Toothpaste, c. ages ago!

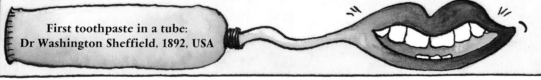

First toothpaste in a tube: Dr Washington Sheffield, 1892, USA

The Romans made their toothpaste from wine vinegar and pumice stone.

ROWLAND HILL:
Postage Stamp, 1840, Britain

Delivery will cost you: 3 sheep, 2 hens and a fish.

No: 1 sheep, 3 hens and a dormouse My final offer!

The Ancient Egyptians had a postal service by 2000 BC, but no stamps!

EARLE DICKSON:
Plasters, 1920, USA

I'm all cut up!

As you see, I had to do something!

Earle invented plasters for his accident-prone wife.

CLARENCE BIRDSEYE:
Frozen Food, 1924, USA

Frozen food!

What's new about that?

GEORGE DE MESTRAL:
Velcro, 1956, Switzerland

It was these tight-clinging cocklebur seeds that gave me the idea!

Persiste little see

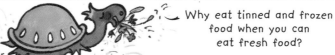

Why eat tinned and frozen food when you can eat fresh food?

People are addicted to gadgetry.

CAN OF WORMS

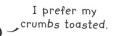
Sliced bread: 1928, USA

I prefer my crumbs toasted.

Pop-up toaster: Charles Strite, 1926, USA

Computer games: Will Higginbotham, 1959, USA

MASARU IBUKA:
Personal Stereo, 1979, Japan

Even parents have them!

RANDOLPH SMITH and KENNETH HOUSE:
Smoke Alarm, 1969, USA

WAA! WAA!

Oops, I'm on fire!

Every day that noise saves thousands of lives!

STEVE JOBS and STEPHEN WOZNIAK:
Personal Computer, 1977, USA

Small, fast computers were made possible by the invention of integrated circuits or silicon chips, which were first built in 1958 and 1959 by JACK KILBY and ROBERT NOYCE, USA.

All I need is an air-current to play on.

Yeah, I'm a real high flyer!

GIDEON SUNDBACK:
Zip, 1913, USA

First invented by Whitcomb Judson in 1893. But it didn't work then, and if you ask me, it doesn't work now ... OUCH!

TIM BERNERS-LEE:
World Wide Web, 1990, Britain

Tim's computer program called "Enquire Within Upon Everything" allowed everyone to use the Internet with just a click of a mouse.

DOUG ENGELBART:
Computer Mouse, 1965, USA

Eeeek!

HUBERT BOOTH:
Vacuum Cleaner, 1901, Britain

Thanks to Mr Booth, kids do their chores and have time to put their feet up.

Up! Up! Up!

ALESSANDRO DI SPINA and SALVINO DEGLI ARMATI:
Spectacles, c.1280, Italy

All the better to see you with, my dear!

Telescope: Hans Lippershey, 1608, Netherlands

Microscope: Hans and Zacharias Janssen, c.1600, Netherlands

PETER HENLEIN:
Watch, 1500, Germany

BEFORE	AFTER
So lovely to see you.	You're late!

Button, c.1235, Germany

Oops, a lost button!

BELL TELEPHONE LABS:
Mobile Phone, 1947, USA

Was there life before the mobile phone?

Are you crazy? Of course not!

Metal Coins, c.640 BC, Lydia (Ancient Turkey)

A coin for your thoughts!

KARL BENZ: Motor Car, 1885, Germany

Faster!

Left a bit.

Too late!

In 1888, Mrs Benz borrowed her husband's tricycle-car without permission! She drove over 120 km; it was the first long distance journey by car.

EDWARD NAIME:
Eraser, 1770, Britain
I'm nothing without you!

I'm nothing without you!

ARISTOPHANES of Byzantium:
Punctuation, c.200 BC

Brilliant! *:;-,

BARDEEN, BRATTAIN and SHOCKLEY:
Transistor, 1948, USA

A transistor is an electronic device used as a switch to control or amplify an electric current. Without it, many modern gadgets would not be possible.

Mirror, c.2500 BC, Ancient Egypt

Mirror, mirror, on the wall...

Best not to ask!

Telescope, microscope, spectacles – I'm still as blind as a bat!

Strange!

I think I'll be a full stop when I grow up!

Well, you'd never make an exclamation mark!

Not a very kind remark!

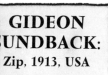

19

Antonio Meucci was a wealthy and successful Italian inventor living in Cuba. In 1849, while he was trying out a new electrotherapy device on a friend, he heard him cry out from an adjoining room. The sound had been carried along the wires. He realized that he had discovered a way to transmit the human voice.

A year later, Antonio and his wife, Esther, left Cuba for Staten Island, USA.

Here Antonio worked on many inventions, including the one he called his "telettrofono".

But he soon began to run out of money, partly because he was so generous to fellow Italians.

Antonio had set up a telettrofono between his house and workshop so his wife could call him in an emergency. In 1860, he demonstrated the system to local journalists and wealthy businessmen. He hoped to raise money to develop it.

Thanks for ... giving us ... somewhere new ... to perch! thank you!

Great invention, old buddy!

But I was hoping for a little investment. *Fancy lunch?*

What if someone steals my idea? *We'll have lost everything.* House SOLD

But Antonio's English was weak and he could not persuade anyone to back his invention.

Worse still, he was now so poor he could not afford to register a patent to protect his idea.

Not the telettrofono? *I'm sorry, my sweet, there was no other way. You were hurt and I was starving.*

I'm sure it will work. *Looks interesting.*

Then he was injured in an explosion, and Esther sold his telephone models to pay his medical bills.

When he recovered, Antonio quickly made another prototype and asked the Great Western Union telegraph company for permission to test it on their telegraph wires.

Just leave it with us, sir. *Of course we haven't forgotten!* *No decision yet, sir.* *Maybe next week!* *Come back tomorrow!* *He's busy today.*

Appointment, sir? *Not in!* *I'm busy!* *Come back after Thanksgiving.* *We meant next Thanksgiving!* *It's lost!*

They kept the prototype and promised to get back to him. But they never did. Antonio visited their offices almost every week for two years. Finally, he was told that the prototype was lost.

Meanwhile, other inventors were catching Antonio up. One was a Scotsman, Alexander Graham Bell.

The boy's a genius! *Faster! Faster!* A MACHINE FOR DEHUSKING WHEAT

A genius! A genius! *How are you, Grandmother?* *A talking dog! Whatever next?*

As a child, Alexander was interested in inventing and in his father's work as a teacher of the deaf.

Alexander experimented with teaching his pet dog to speak by manipulating its vocal chords. He was quite successful!

Can I have a talking dog?

Sorry, not at home ... please leave a message.

It cost about $250 to secure a patent – a lot of money in the 1870s.

The patent holder was responsible for stopping others from "borrowing" his invention.

Who'd be an inventor?

Me – I'd invent the never-ending worm.

Slurp!

Inventors invent, birds chirp; it's the way of the world.

By the time he was 26, Alexander and his family had moved to Canada.

Alexander later went on to tutor teachers of deaf people in Boston, USA. Here he met his future wife, Mabel Hubbard.

Alexander called his first machine a "harmonic telegraph."

Alexander spent his spare time trying to invent a telephone, but without much success.

Then Mabel's father gave him money to employ a technician called Tom Watson.

The first telephones worked on private circuits from house to house.

Alexander and Tom experimented with different speech machines day and night.

On 14 February 1876, Mabel's father felt they were close to success and registered a patent.

By the 1880s, over 50,000 Americans owned telephones!

On 10 March, their big moment came. Alexander talked into their latest transmitter and Tom heard him on a receiver in the other room. Their telephone worked!

Slurp!

A tortoise can no more help not inventing than he can help not thinking.

Thinking is not like eating – you don't have to think to live.

Your humble inventor, ma'am.

We are most impressed, Professor Bell.

Alexander quickly started work on improving his model and on selling the idea. He even travelled to England to demonstrate his telephone to Queen Victoria.

I protest!

Mr Bell, the telephone is my invention.

My dear chap, you're mistaken.

No, not mistaken ...

but defeated.

But not everyone was happy. Antonio Meucci was sure that his idea had been stolen. He protested through the newspapers and in the courts until he died in poverty in 1889.

Bell made the first long-distance call in 1892.

You'll be talking mobile phones next!

Telephone call for you, Daddy!

Hello ... hello...

Help, Grand-mama!

Take that thing out of my office! The way to communicate is by letter.

There were other cases too. There was even one against the Great Western Union, who had employed Thomas Edison to make a telephone system for them. Alexander began to tire of the time he had to spend on protecting his patent. In 1879, now rich and famous, he went back to helping deaf students and inventing this and that.

Mobile phones: 1947

After you.

No, after you.

No, I insist!

Allow me!

Together?

Together!

ENTER

INVENTORS' HALL OF FAME

A new twist to the story came in 2002, when the US Congress decided that the true inventor of the telephone was Antonio Meucci. But many people still believe that it was Alexander's enthusiasm for the telephone, as well has his ability to communicate, that convinced people that it was a great idea.

What's an inventor without money?

A forgotten inventor.

Tring, tring, tring!

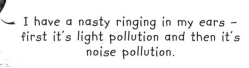

I have a nasty ringing in my ears – first it's light pollution and then it's noise pollution.

THREE ZOOMS FOR WILBUR (1867–1912) AND ORVILLE (1871–1948) WRIGHT AND THEIR FABULOUS FLYING MACHINE

As children, Wilbur and Orville Wright loved to make and invent things – especially things that flew. In their home town, Dayton, Ohio, in the USA, they earned pocket money by selling their creations.

Later, they opened a bicycle shop together. Bicycles were just becoming popular, and they grew skilled at repairing and building them.

When they read about the death of the pioneer glider Otto Lillienthal in 1896, they became determined to build their own flying machine!

After much research they built a glider and flew it – as a kite! Then they started planning a glider that could carry a person.

In 1900 and 1901, they tested two full-sized gliders but neither was a success. The brothers almost gave up.

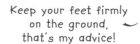

24

WIND TUNNEL NOTES

The faster that air moves across the wing, the less it presses the wing down. Good wing shape means there is more pressure below – so the wing goes up!

Instead, they went back to their workshop, built a wind tunnel and tested different wing shapes.

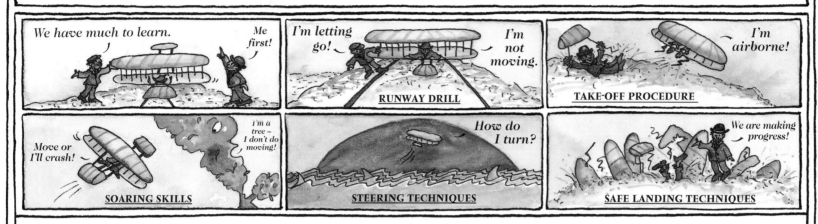

Their third glider was a great success and the brothers made nearly a thousand glides in it. Then they started to build their first powered aeroplane with its own engine and propellers.

By the end of 1903, they were ready. On 17 December, at Kill Devil Hill, near Kitty Hawk, North Carolina, Orville launched himself into the air in their aeroplane, *Flyer 1*, and flew for 12 seconds. It was the first powered flight ever!

First steam-powered "flying leap": Clement Ader, 1890, France

ZOOM ZOOM!

Not bad for fledgling flyers.

They'll never do it!

I think they might!

But how does it fly without flapping its wings?

It has propellers turned by an engine that push it forward.

25

Over the next two years, Wilbur and Orville built two more planes, improving their designs all the time. By 1905, *Flyer 3* could stay in the air for over 30 minutes, turning and looping at speeds of up to 35 mph.

Then in 1908, after signing a contract with the US War Department, Wilbur toured France and America to demonstrate their invention. In New York, he flew around the Statue of Liberty to the amazement of the crowds below. Wilbur and Orville had conquered the air!

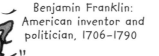
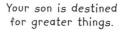
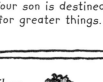

Viva, Guglielmo Marconi
(1874–1937) and his Radio

PING!
POW!
ZAP!

Mr Franklin will now prove that lightning has electric power!

Clever boy!

A spell in the Navy is what you need, my boy.

Grr!

As a boy, Guglielmo irritated his Italian father by pretending to be the scientist Benjamin Franklin and experimenting with the power of lightning.

Listen, Mama, I can make the bell ring without wires!

Late one night...

Radio Waves

Radio Waves

BE QUIET! I'm trying to sleep.

Is it magic, dear?

WOOF?

PING!

BATTERY   SPARK PRODUCER

TRANSMITTER

BATTERY

RECEIVER

Then he read about the work of Heinrich Hertz on electromagnetic waves. Guglielmo realized that the waves could be used to send messages without a wire between the sender, the transmitter and the receiver. He became completely absorbed by the idea and repeated Hertz's experiments many times at home.

Are you waving or playing?

Shhh, pet, I'm resting!

Silly nonsense, be QUIET!

Ah, gunshot. He's heard my signal!

BANG!

AERIAL

TAP-TAP-TAP!

Be QUIET!

His brother, Alfonso, helped. He would wait in their garden with a receiver and wave a handkerchief when he received messages sent by Guglielmo from the attic.

Soon, Guglielmo was sending messages to Alfonso over long distances.

What are radio waves and what do they do?

James Maxwell discovered them in 1864; Heinrich Hertz produced them in 1883.

They carry signals, such as sounds, through the air at the speed of light!

Through the air? Like us?

Yes, but invisibly!

Scary!

The human need to communicate is a mystery that I will not venture to explore.

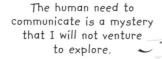

BURP!

Crumbs! Will it be wireless telephones next? Where will I perch?

Did you mention crumbs?

Many more crumbs and you'll need the Wright brothers to get you airborne!

He tried to interest the Italian Post Office in his experiments but they were not interested.

Guglielmo set sail for England where the Post Office gave him money and technical help.

His experiments went well and in 1897, he had founded the *Wireless Telegraph and Signal Company Ltd*. They were producing radios by 1898. In 1909, when the *SS Republic* collided with another ship, a radio message meant that almost all the passengers were saved, over 1,700 people.

Guglielmo returned to Italy a hero. Before long, new uses were found for radio waves helped by the invention of valves that made it easier to detect and transmit radio waves clearly. In the 1920s, radio stations such as the BBC started entertainment broadcasting but Guglielmo was not impressed. He wanted his wireless radio to save lives at sea and thought all other uses frivolous.

We all need a helping hand at times.

First transatlantic signal: Guglielmo Marconi, 1901, Italy

In 1898, Queen Victoria used wireless radio to communicate with the Royal yacht.

The wireless telegraph saved its first life at sea in 1899.

SPLASH!

Can I have a radio? Can I, can I?

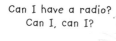

Dream on!

29

Tune in for JOHN LOGIE BAIRD (1888–1946) and the TV BOYS

John Logie Baird was fascinated by new inventions. While still a schoolboy, he connected his house in Scotland to his friends' houses with a home-made telephone exchange (although the wires that he hung across the road were a little too low!). Later, his interest turned to television.

John was determined to be the first to make a working television. But the system he chose was very different to the electronic TV of today. His system was mechanical and used huge spinning disks to generate a tiny picture. He had no money and so had to build it in his kitchen out of old junk.

Sometimes the disks span out of control, showering the room with glass and metal. But John did not give up.

In 1925, in a London department store, he became the first person to demonstrate a mechanical television.

30

Shame it didn't work out for John.

A year later, a group of scientists queued up outside John's tiny kitchen to watch him demonstrate his TV system. They loved it and soon John was able to persuade the British Broadcasting Corporation to show experimental TV programmes.

I thought of it when I was ploughing.

Interesting, Son, but it's home time now.

CAMERA   AERIAL   RECEIVER   IMAGE

I showed Sir my TV idea.

Interesting, Son, but these 'ere 'ens need feeding.

The first TV screens were only postcard-sized.

But, unfortunately for John, the mechanical system was not as good as the electronic system that other inventors were working on at the same time. Philo T. Farnsworth, a farmer's son from Utah, USA, was the first person to put forward an electronic system in 1922, when he was only 14 years old.

First regular TV broadcasts: 1939, USA

BEWARE OF THE DOG!

First colour TV system: Peter Goldmark, 1940, USA

It was Japanese inventor Kenjiro Takayanagi who demonstrated the first fully electronic televisions in 1926. But the inventor who helped make TV possible was a Russian-American, Vladimir Zworykin, who developed equipment that recorded images and displayed pictures. This was the birth of television as we know it today! By the 1950s, TV sets were starting to appear in every home – thanks to the enthusiasm and hard work of these inventors and many others just like them.

Can I have a TV? Can I?

Someone reinvent the Stone Age, please!

Extra Loud Cheer for WOMEN INVENTORS

STEPHANIE KWOLEK: Kevlar, 1966, USA

I'm Robin Hood!

Well, you don't scare me 'cos I'm wearing the Kevlar vest!

Kevlar is an exceptionally strong plastic material. Used in radial tyres and knife- and bullet-proof vests, it has saved MANY lives!

BEULAH HENRY: Snap-on Umbrella Cover and other inventions, 1912–1970, USA

You'll always make a splash with a Beulah 'brella!

Beulah held 49 patents and is known as "Lady Edison" in the USA.

MELITTA BENTZ: Coffee Filter Papers, 1908, Germany

No more coffee dregs for me!

Why not patent the idea?

AYME BALL: Preserved Saffron, 1637, Britain

Take ye the stigmas of ye olde crocus flowers and dissolve into tincture.

Never mind ye olde saffron, where's ye olde bone!

Ayme Ball was a widow when she became the first woman to be granted her own patent.

REBECCA CHING: Worm-destroying Lozenge, 1796, Britain

They wriggle ...

and squiggle ...

inside you!

Until they took Ching lozenges!

Lots of people used to have worms.

QUEEN LEIZU: Silk, c. 3200 BC, China

Spin this unravelled silkworm cocoon.

If you want to live, give the credit to the queen!

In early times, if you wanted to be known as a female inventor it helped to be a queen.

SARAH E. GOODE: Folding Cabinet Bed, 1885, USA

But we need to go to bed.

Just one more letter, my love

Snore!

Sarah was the first African-American woman to receive a patent in the USA.

32

I thought necessity was the mother of invention.

Some inventions are downright frivolous.

Thank you, frivolous inventors!

ROSE MITCHTOM:
Teddy Bear, 1902, USA

Are you a honey bee?

No, I'm your president.

MARGARETE STEIFF:
Teddy Bear, 1902, Germany

For you, Auntie!

This will make a great cuddly toy.

SOPHIA BARNACLE:
Helter-skelter, 1907, Britain

WEE!

WOOAH!

ZOOM!

FASTER!

Me, me! My go!

Is it safe?

A PENNY A TURN!

Both Rose and Margarete have a claim to the teddy bear. Rose named hers after the US president "Teddy" Roosevelt, when he refused to shoot a baby bear. Margarete's was based on a nephew's drawing.

The teddy bear is one of the most popular toys ever invented.

Has anyone invented a birdie-bear?

Another bird-brain!

If my mum had used a Snugli, I might have grown into a dove!

Even a Snugli can't work miracles!

Unlike women inventors and owl brains!

SARAH MATHER:
Submarine Telescope and Lamp, 1845 and 1870, USA

Blistering barnacles, if only I'd had a Sarah Mather telescope!

ANN MOORE:
Snugli, 1969, USA

Translated, that means "I want a Snugli."

Waaa!

Coo-coo!

Ann invented the Snugli after a visit to West Africa.

The telescope and lamp allowed vessels to survey the ocean depths.

ISABELLA CUNIO:
Woodblock Engraving, c. 1200, Italy

Brother, let's carve the exploits of Alexander into wood, then dip them in ink and print them.

OK, but only if I take the credit, 'cos I'm the boy!

MARY ANDERSON:
Windscreen-wiper, 1903, USA

Maybe I should invent a windscreen-wiper.

Keep on wiping!

It is likely that Isabella made the first known woodblock engravings with her twin, Alex.

My life is one long helter-skelter.

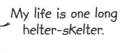

Oh yes, dear, it's all go for a tortoise!

33

And Finally, My Favourite Inventors, Take a Bow

Or a curtsy!

What about balls?

Who invented balls?

Balls: an unknown Stone-Age child, c. 40,000 BC

You made that up.

It is what you call an ill-informed guess.

He needs an encyclopedia.

Encyclopedia: Abdul Farah, 1270 BC, Syria

FRANCES GABE:
Self-cleaning House, 1950, USA

Everything got washed in Frances's house: dishes, books, even the dog!

JAN VAN EYCK:
Oil Paints, c. 1410, Flanders

These are some of my best colours!

Watercolour paints, invented by the Chinese in c. 900 AD, are brilliant too.

UNKNOWN DUTCH INVENTOR:
Roller Skates, c. 1700

Don't st playin

In 1760, Joseph Merlin wore a pair to a ball in London. While playing the violin, he crashed into a mirror!

JOHN STARLEY:
Safety Bicycle, 1885, Britain

Bikes came in all shapes until I invented the safety bike!

The first known bicycle was invented in 1817, by Baron von Drais of Germany.

JOHAN VAALER:
Paper Clip, 1899, Norway

A small, but perfect, design.

JOHN MONTAGU, FOURTH EARL OF SANDWICH:
The Sandwich, 1762, Britain

YUM!   *YUM!*

WALTER HUNT:
Modern Safety Pin, 1849, USA

An Ancient Egyptian invented the first safety pin, of course!

ANCIENT ROMAN:
Cross-bladed Scissors, c. ages ago! (c. 100 A

Perfect for cutting toenails or paper or hair or cheese or...

RICHARD KNERR and ARTHUR MERLIN:
First Plastic Hula Hoop, 1958, USA

A toy that came from Ancient Egypt.

LU PAN:
Kite, c. 400 BC, China

OLE KIRK CHRISTIANSEN:
Lego, 1955, Denmark

I made it myself!

My favourite invention is my shell.

I'm with you, Dad – "Forever inwards" is my motto.

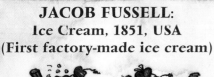

JACOB FUSSELL:
Ice Cream, 1851, USA
(First factory-made ice cream)

LISS!

Double bliss!

he first ice cream may have been
ade in Persia about 100 BC.

CONRAD GESNER:
Pencil, 1565, Germany

WILL YOU BE

MINE?

WOOF?

Me?

Conrad invented a wood and
graphite pencil, but English
shepherds first wrote with graphite.

CHRISTIAN BERNHARD TAUCHNITZ:
Paperback Book, 1841, Germany

You can smell them,

hug them,

and chuck them!

read them ...

First pop-up book: c. 1856, England

Celluloid for making film: John Hyatt, 1870, USA

ADOLPHE SAX:
Saxophone, 1846, Belgium

It has a wicked sound!

JOHN WALKER:
Matches, 1827, Britain

Well, it beats rubbing two sticks together!

GLAMOROUS WOMEN OF ANCIENT EGYPT:
Cosmetics, c. 3000 BC

More rouge, I think, slave.

Mistress, you are divinely rouged!

JOSEPH N. NIEPCE:
Photography, 1826, France

How long will it take?

Only eight hours!

By 1839, Louis Daguerre from France
and William Fox-Talbot from
England had developed systems
that improved on Joseph's process.

First pocket camera: 1895, USA

First photo of me: 2005, nest

MARVIN STONE:
rinking Straw, 1888, USA

drink is
omplete
ithout
one!

OWEN MACLAREN:
Baby Buggy, 1965, Britain

Q: Why a baby buggy?
A: Because it has a baby in it!

FRANÇOIS LOUIS CAILLER:
First Chocolate Bar, 1819, Switzerland

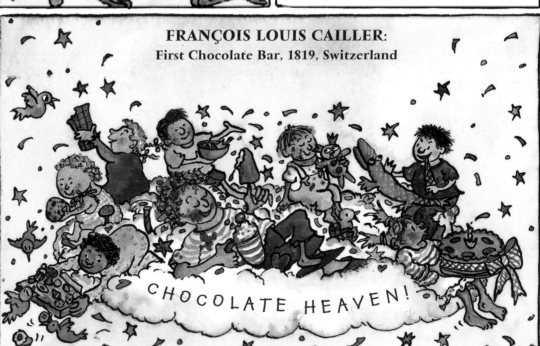

CHOCOLATE HEAVEN!

Hernan Cortes was the Spanish explorer who brought the cocoa
bean to Europe from Mexico in 1519. It was the start of all
things chocolate! Thank you, Hernan!

This author may be a chocolate freak!

There's no maybe about it!

Index of Inventors

Index of Inventions

HIP,

hip,

GOODBYE!

hip ...

WALKER BOOKS BY MARCIA WILLIAMS

The Iliad and the Odyssey

Greek Myths

King Arthur and the Knights of the Round Table

The Adventures of Robin Hood

Mr William Shakespeare's Plays

Bravo, Mr William Shakespeare!

Charles Dickens and Friends

The Canterbury Tales

God and His Creations

Three Cheers for Inventors!